Moonshine @11

Rajya Lakshmi

ISBN 978-93-5458-518-0
© Rajya Lakshmi 2021
Published in India 2021 by Pencil

A brand of
One Point Six Technologies Pvt. Ltd.
123, Building J2, Shram Seva Premises,
Wadala Truck Terminal, Wadala (E)
Mumbai 400037, Maharashtra, INDIA
E connect@thepencilapp.com
W www.thepencilapp.com

DISCLAIMER: *The opinions expressed in this book are those of the authors and do not purport to reflect the views of the Publisher.*

Author biography

poetry is a passion and purpose

CONTENTS

Epigraph

As above and so below

Foreword

It is dedicated to all souls that seek happiness

Preface

The real adventures in life

Acknowledgements

I want to thank all the poetry writers around the world
grateful for the words of poetry

Power in you sun

The creations of you
Is tightened to bring to
Heal the hearts of the world
The hearts that suffered
Travels in time if space
A wisp of sternly
And immortal moments
Struck the minds
And shimmer of
Thousands of suns with
A golden glow of silence

12

Passion

The passion and it's
Influence and the things
Which shows in which it
Is always return to back at its light
And it's available to the source
And king of your life who makes
You feel alive again learn to stay
Patient

Brighter life

We can go the switch that
Connects light within you and onto you, we have it and the
back of us shows love with heart and finally together
happy faces.
Be touch you when you
Match the same dream,
And spirit is filled with tenderness
And led it to its thirst of
Spring which fed fantasies
And explode the moments of
Captivating gaze heart goes
With you, just beginning and
Aim for the moon, what you see
With eyes will happen, someone,
Somewhere feels as you feel you
Will be in this world.
See the universe in galaxies,
In your hands to seek the things
Which set your soul on fire,
It is your world that you see
And the way is also that you can
Make it happier and brighter
I was in your hands.

Be you

You are a beautiful soul needed to be preserved
to come into existence to live into your own
Truths to light other worlds by you
You can be the one whoo sort out
Problems

mindset

have a light of hope
goes in a way that lead others
a strategy that has a will
and a way to the solutions
will be found if you search
with stay to that which keeps
you safe when you are side
of it the strength you attained
after stroms the more you
give to it the more it gives
the real strenght in you

come out of sorrows

stand by the one who motivates you
in the right direction that gives you
smiles and teaches how to smile
you are the own better you
be with the one who always brings
the best in you

Paradise

Break the mould
Be you Heaven like a
Cloud there's a sky with
You and I was there
With you like away
And hope to a dream
Always be ease to
Your life and find your
Own paradise
In which you belong

New diemensions

I try to be different I try
To be someone else, I love
The people that I get along with
I am floating away and I am lost
In my own space my own eyes
Started teasing me, skies and moments captured and excited to see the unity in everything that combines divine still together I take
Some adventure decision even ends if I am stupid and also be it I am
Reserved.
Amazing feels something have a strong impact which makes you stronger be more on track you,
A wise and heart-mind faith
A new way to think to master
A new way to be,
Explore the new reality of you.

Always have you

Setting the fire within every moment unleashing the vibes
and the new versions play on the act to
Turn the things on the edge which
Is kept in dark, warrior formulated
Battle chaos yet order and
Welder twist winning over battles
I will find a way
And get adapted to
Pure bliss and foundation
Is strong and work for you
And shall get you there.
The seed has started its raising
It's turned to glow like a star in
The sky you are seeing to get
In the process of growth and
Finally, reach what is meant for
Found a thing in which I look,
For outside of me, and
Back to me finally getting
Cosy and has already became
Better in which moonshine
Has more mean to me.

Walking with you

I am the picture in the clouds,
Reflection of water and the face
In every flower you see,
The power is going to help you
Which comes to you from the skies
Above and it's bliss that senses
And directs you in its way,
Towards a pure love.
And with the spirit of fire
And grateful for what I got,
The passion and its influence
And the things in which it shows
In which always return to
Back at it the light which is
Source and made to believe
It is the king of your life
And this feeling makes me
 Alive again which is in the hands
Of someone and finally
Learn to stay patient
And can face everything
With balance
Good vibes only

Knocking

Someone is knocking at dreams,
In which you are becoming it
Living you're with
There's a fallen angel living
With great heart and a happy face
And someone speaking
You are brave and giving
Hope to you live again
And a heart is about to beat
Faster and all things are
Eventually falling apart. how
Lucky are you
Parts of me and him
Together carry as complete
The rainbow which exists in colours
And a new whispering of
Sun rising at new dawns of
Miracles and mysteries.

Stardust

I think its time to smile
Too many stars and too
Many dreams we seek
And the reality is in front
Of these things, I am a speck
Of these things of stardust
If you chase anything. Chase that
Excited to be a lot more you
Time has come for the kingdom,
The sights that we will run
Into a pattern in which you
Have a lot of space and
Piece for your wanderings
Of soul.

Artist and it's mirror

To define you
You are an art and I am
Artist, you are the reason
For many of us to believe
In dreams and most of the
Happier and crazier moments
I have them because of you.
No matter which phase are
You in,life is a fairy tale
It' s like an ocean which
Is held upon the mirror image
And it is the love beyond
All the things from
Mine to yours
Just looking at you.

Designer

Discover the better
Designer to
Be someone of me
That can complete me
And living dreams and
Never giving up
Finding solutions who
Pulls your work and see it
Through you

Real bliss

The love that comes without ego
And it can be seen through
Your soul and you look at the world
With someone eyes and
Celebrate the evolving you
A mirror is your soul
It gives whatever your want
It shares it's light to heal you
In which you find things to
Laugh wholeheartedly.
Raise your awareness to
Your own wings and carries you
A flow of guard

Shiny heavens

There's a hero
The special one who is masked
Waiting for your arrival
It's you who come back.
As a most daring person
The better you
The universe is in your favour
Catch the magic and
It keys hold and have
Them in your hands
And I wanna see you
Stand-in storms
Go with the love which
Awaits for you in
A land of fairies which
Keeps on falling for you
In forms like a shooting star

Journey and space

It's time for the vision and focuses
To bring and let it flow through.
You and transform and ride
And the journey through your life
Be a superhero of your own story
And that connects its dots
To your dream travel. let the freedom of fire rise in you
And keep the space in you
For me, that roots me and
Grows me up and have a
Listing of things to be done

Existence

I am the soul that only can live with
You
I am your mind
I am your madness... I am
The secret in your eyes
I am the first who knows the meaning of live with you

Cycles

Embrace the moments the
Magic of chimes of a magical
Wheel chart of unchanged
Destiny and a campaign with
You and a soft light candle
In the temple and soothing
The vibration of holy shrines
In which you whispered in
Heart and soul and my darling
Of heavenly beauty

The strings of life

It is a string of a flow of
Music that surrounds me to
You and you to me,
It is always in alignment
That takes me towards you,
Like a falling of stars
Keeps on shining
For you and me.
There is a voice in the air.
Which makes the rose of blossom.
Being whispered in my soul
Since there I have been
In love.

Patterns

Eyes hold a conversation and
Get lost to a place
Where you swing freely a mere moments the place
Where you stand and can
Access the power and
Broke its patterns and
Create a new one
In a protective shield
In which you are delighted.

Seasons and it's views

Like a puzzle the now you
You can see your path
Clearly as if the truth
And now can lead
Only for you the one who
Makes a day brighter
The sunrises and sunsets
In different seasons
That I have you indifferent
Moods that makes me
Go through many rising and
Falling and world is seen
In different views and
My dreams are fulfilled
Like easy

Weapons

We are all made of standard
You are the bringer of the changes
That is needed to be in order
You are beyond in everything
And you are formless and you are
Divine that takes many forms
To reach me that extends
Like sky with vastness,
With it's limitless features
To cope with weapons
In survival mode

Blessings

To this life, everything has you
You define the love that
Can turn the soul undergo
Into various mysteries
Magic just arrived
And show its play
To the one who always special,
That leads your soul
Cleansed to be pure

Change

A power that has to be in forms
Always onwards and upwards
Change the way in you
Are living and go with the one
Who is good for you
And off blue skies and her
Glam and you were out of
Your mind

Maagic

To this life, everything has you
You define the love that
Can turn the soul undergo
Into various mysteries
Magic just arrived
And show its play
To the one who always special,
That leads your soul
Cleansed to be pure.
Always onwards and upwards

Side of you

I have a new energy and the
Strength brings and stands for
I became the name of sounds
Which walk with me in
My journey and breathing dreams
Like air the more you were today
In which you were rooted by a power where you can stand
firm

Hums

I can now face my battles
You are a guide that brings me
Here so far in which I was
Proud of in which I have.
Some focus on me and
Gazes on merely admiring steps
And the tunes of yesterday's
Year

Decidings

You are the writer of my life
And which is designed to be at the pace
And that is needed to be lightened
You were my forever lucky fallen
Star and journey to my success
And wandering thoughts you have
Painted in me to seek it

Colours of life

All your sayings in various colours
So whatever maybe
Your beloved colour and I
Will still find me in the garden
Of roses and like water in the mirage that is reflected in
the
Moon, you are within everything
You are hearing that everything
Is known to you

Just be

Heavens can't wait
And I am watching
You was starting at skies with
Joy listen to every depth
Of worlds it's you
You are the breath
Of all breaths
You are the universe.

Moments

You are always at the moments
In which you search and
Run for what you want
And in which ready to go there
And by through your
Efforts in which you
Ride at different situations
To the one eternal bliss

Seek

You are the seeker
In which you continue
It at every moment
And you are constant
Endeavour in which one
It is revealed to itself
And other is connected
To infinity and it exists everywhere

Vibes

You are the vibe that
Gives fragrance and
Remains current to
The court of heart
And flow through it.
When time comes
Exercise whatever comes
Shapes you and moulds you
Which cleanses me
And teaches me
Show me your plans,

You and me

You are the potter
And I am the clay
The space is within the heart
Is as vast as the universe for you
The bringer if heavens to this
Earth all there and and I was with
You so keeps the watch all day and night

Deeper

All times evokes hidden
Emotions of mind
And story of angelic life
In blessed midroyals
Are born to rule and
Conquer where kings
And queens were born
As guided night as bright
And for well being of joy
Reflected in life

I see you

Eyes of a brilliant blue
And a face that stays within
My heart, and parts of yourself
To the most Inner being and
Mind full of matters and eyes
See the endless Monday blues
And the truth is in the name of love
And the nectar is falling
And the pictures that are
Seen in the mirror of heart,
And calls by looking into eyes

learning the process

It is mysterious and
Seeing it in the eyes of
Soul, and filled with gems
Of true love and whistled in
The afternoon and in the name
Of love sometimes and feel
Lonely and some hearts
Carried to the moon and they are
Hosts left to mend themselves
And ready to dance down the
Earth and after learn the art
Of floating

49

Framing

Feeling connected by someone
And who shows the real realities
And always felt like lucky me
To have those who have a concern
And make them appear as new ones that is designed with
more.
Framework

Directions

Surrounded by stars
And a dark blue sky
And stay wide awake
And we are all the seeds
That become closer to golden light
A deep life-giving love
That is enriched gives you the essence
In a limitless ocean and that's all
Been and the very thought of
You made me smiles

Sights of you

Designed for you
To appear there
And for you to go there
And keep doing which you were
Keep on the hustle and burn your inner pains to become
the water
Of purity

52

Hustle

Designed for you
To appear there
And for you to go there
And keep doing which you were
Keep on the hustle and burn your inner pains to become
the water
Of purity

53

Divine soul

He goes before and
Behind the eyes
Of the grace and activation
And I found you brilliant
And a mountain the divine strength
Stays latent in you
And move upward
And will come amazing miracles

The wind

You are the seek
That can go into its growth
And made existence into
Reality and you are the base
The wind that guides
That Is too deep and fully
To understand and a dandelion
In your hand that keeps you hungry
And of the division seeing my shadow next to yours he's
the breeze they cling to,

Searchings

Searching for you
All the way you were at
Every moment of me
In every choice and through every joy and brought me
here in which
I am grateful for
I gave you my heart and locked you
In it my soul is to keep you
I have been watching you.
New heights are awaiting you are on your journey I am the
sign
Of the letter and the designation of it

Hearings

Life is a shout out to
Genuine happiness that is
Flying fast through space in
Desires destination and leaves it's
Firey mark that keeps you moving
And keeps on communicating
With you to be safe I together have
The vision of the heart.
Be it the earth I gave you my day
And night to explore chasing our
Tails to see you in smiles which makes my heartache. I
flow away with holy waters and end of the rhyme we can
take the trials on

57

Sky wandering

I feel you through my soul
You fill in me like endless love
You were the precious soul
That creates new directions in me
I was reborn every day you are   a   beautiful flame, just
Like clouds a deep understanding in you, you are fast as an
infinite ocean has capacity to enter a tiny drop

Made in

Thoughts are tightly wrapped
Up knowing fully well
The origin and the design
Of all the things and give a smiles
Of full moon as peace and a praise
The train of spirit is a beautiful
Feeling and a fountain of honesty

Hall of flames

Curious eyes carried you
Lightly to the other side
And a plenty of beautiful passing
If the tides I have got something you should see a sacred
beetle
The chorus needs to sing.
Let it happen to stay in the mind
Sky and my mind is built on me
That you have done thunderstorms in cold weather

Beyond the pace

You were on the nice things.
Happened to me started to live in the moments now I can
make choices up to my heart and patterns that come up to
that are present in the cosmos the bliss we enjoy is eternal
infinity that we thrive for

The ocean

Wonders in the life of a full state of living and rely on the path that we take and prevailing of choices and I am captive of it and side by side we shall have it together with the commands and its realms you tucked away inside me to the dimple and echoes of goodness in my heart

62

Chilling more

Become the one with warriors the moments
we claim and attain a glimpse of chances
to reach the place for all playful and
compassionate things get there and live a little celebrate by
gathering as one

Homelandd

You are the rider of your journey
To go for a homeland
Where you find more straightway
And more incense that burns up
To be in your own choices
And creations that you explore yourself

Finally at you

It is the way you present in me
That no one ever would
The way to go heaven
Is with an idea having the
The bliss that sees you
And framed you in
The flow of things in joys
That put you in blessings
As dreams to come true.